Brother James

The Rose and the Lily

The Twin Sisters

Brother James

The Rose and the Lily
The Twin Sisters

ISBN/EAN: 9783744686365

Printed in Europe, USA, Canada, Australia, Japan

Cover: Foto ©Thomas Meinert / pixelio.de

More available books at **www.hansebooks.com**

H. McGRATH, PHILADELPHIA.

THE

ROSE AND THE LILY;

OR,

The Twin Sisters.

By BROTHER JAMES.

PHILADELPHIA:

HENRY McGRATH,

No. 733 MARKET STREET,

1864.

THE

ROSE AND THE LILY.

CHAPTER I.

LAURENCE MACMULLEN was a hard-working and industrious mechanic, who had been left a widower at the early age of thirty, with two daughters, who were twins, to support.

Unlike what twins are in general, these little girls differed exceedingly in personal appearance, and nearly as much in disposition and character. Aileen, the eldest, was florid, robust, full of life, spirit, and activity, whilst May, the younger, was mild, delicate, and retiring, without being positively shy. Their father was a master-carpenter by trade, and, as his avocations required him to be a great deal from home, he was

obliged to trust the guardian-
ship of his children to another,
who was partly a servant and
partly a friend. So far as pu-
rity of life and conduct went,
he could not have chosen a
better than Kitty Neill, in
whose character the only
drawbacks were, an easiness
of temper which suffered itself to be swayed by those
whom she loved, and a love
of story-telling and absurd
speculations regarding the future, in which it is at all times

useless, and sometimes dangerous, to engage. From an early period, Kitty had distinguished the children committed to her charge by the names of "the Rose" and "the Lily,"—the former of which designations was applied to Aileen, the latter to May; and as the Irish are a poetical people, the applicability of the titles thus foolishly conferred remained with them, since, in point of fact, the elder girl not inaptly por-

trayed the blooming flower
whose name she bore, and the
younger, in the general deli-
cacy of her complexion, and
the quiet, timid, and retiring
nature of her disposition,
might, with equal justness,
be compared to the modest
and unobtrusive lily, that
loves the shade. Although
Kitty loved them both, still
she was proud of Aileen; and
as the little girl's tempera-
ment was more high-spirited
and resolute than that of her

sister, she gradually established a sway over her nurse
which the latter could not
shake off, and thus it hap-
pened that minor faults were
overlooked, and minor short-
comings made light of, until,
at last, Aileen submitted with
the worst possible grace to be
questioned or censured at all.
She was occasionally hasty,
sharp, and short-tempered,
and during her fits of passion
she said and did things which,
if not completely indefensible,

were often the source of much annoyance to the objects of them, and of much sorrow to herself when her better sense returned and showed her how unreasonable she had been. May, on the other hand, was much more easily dealt with; she had always the soft answer ready which "turns away wrath," and was infinitely more inclined to make excuses for others than to require them for herself. In their education, too, the same

difference prevailed : they
went to a day-school kept by
Miss Moriarty, a maiden lady
of advanced years, and whose
only foible was an ardent desire to be considered much
younger than she really was.
Her disposition was excellent,
and her information tolerably
extensive ; but she had once
been handsome, and her father
had once been rich, and now
that in the decline of life she
had lost both beauty and
wealth, unfortunately for her-

self, the recollections connected with them remained, and
made her discontented with
her present lot,—which, after
all, was a comfortable one,—
and led her often very injudi-
ciously to talk of her "down-
fall" before the more favoured
of her scholars, in a repining
and discontented tone, which
sometimes made her the pity,
and quite as often the ridi-
cule, of the younger girls,
who well knew how to depre-
cate her anger, and insure

her good will, by dosing her
with flattery, or listening with
complacency to the details of-
"the conquests" which she
had made in early life, and
the "splendour" in which her
father, " the Captain," used to
live. She never intended to
do harm by such idle stories;
but, nevertheless, they produced evil effects in more ways
than one, by idling the time
of her scholars, by distracting
their young minds into useless
and unprofitable channels of

thought, and by rendering
them in some degree hypo-
crites, inasmuch as, against
their convictions and feelings,
they felt that they must sym-
pathize with her, or lose her
good will. Unfortunately for
Aileen MacMullen, this amiable but eccentric preceptress
early distinguished her in a
particular manner by her regard; and as the little girl
found it easier to flatter her
mistress than to learn her
tasks, she did the former, and

left the latter much more
to chance than she ought to
have done. Among her school-
fellows, also, her decision of
manner and impatience of all
control produced their effects,
and led her to obtain as great
an influence over them as
they did over every one else.
These weaknesses of character—for as yet they were no
more—might have been easily
cured or prevented, but there
was no firm hand to eradicate
the tares, and so she went on,

praised by her schoolmistress, flattered by her nurse, and neglected by her father, who loved her dearly, but was too busily engaged to give her that needful superintendence which was particularly necessary to check the bad consequences of the evil training which she every day received.

She had one true and real friend and adviser in her sister May, who, although the younger of the two, saw the defects in her character, and

would have checked them if
she could. May often pointed
out to her the danger of grow-
ing up in ignorance, and the
still greater danger of listening to the idle adulations of
those who called her pretty
and clever, but who seldom
added the epithet "good" to
the list. She willingly assisted
her in getting her tasks, but
never failed to admonish her
that, although Miss Moriarty
might overlook her backward-
ness, the world would not do

so hereafter; and although Kitty might tolerate her waywardness of temper, she would, at a future day, meet with those who would be more mindful of her faults. For these remonstrances, however, Aileen had always a ready answer.

"I am not afraid of the world," she said, "nor of those I am likely to meet with in it. I cannot help my natural character, or being what I suppose I was intended to be. I

do not wish to do wrong, and
if others think much of me,
I cannot help that, either:
how could I? My father is
satisfied with me, so is Miss
Moriarty, so is Kitty; I can't
be so bad as *you* make me out,
therefore; and when I am, I
shall feel it, and stop short."

"Are you quite sure that
you can do so, dearest Aileen?"
said May; "and even if you
do, is there no danger that
your good resolutions may not
be too late?"

"It is never too late to mend, you know," said "the Rose," laughing; "so just work this weary sum for me, and say no more."

"I will work the sum for you, with pleasure," was May's reply; "but you are wrong to ask me to do so, rather than to do it yourself. If I had been as—as careless as you have been, I could not now assist you; but you will not always be sure of an assistant, dear Aileen, and there-

fore ought to struggle hard
against the spirit that tempts
you to neglect what you ought
to remember, and to remember only what you ought to
forget."

"You are always wiser than
your elders," was the petulant
reply; "and I tell you now,
as I often told you before,
that I would be much obliged
by your keeping your good
advice to yourself. You fancy
yourself remarkably clever,
because I ask you to help

me to do what I could do myself in half an hour, if I only chose to set my mind to it; and I will do it, too,— some time or other; and then we shall see who will get best through the world,—you, with your sleek ways and snail's pace, or I, with my idleness and bad temper, as *you* call it."

"Indeed, you wrong me, Aileen," said poor May, with tears in her eyes; "I only meant to say——"

"You only meant to say

what you *did* say, I suppose,"
interrupted the spoiled girl.
"You only meant to say to
me what no one but yourself
ever ventures to say, and
what nobody *shall* say with
impunity, either, without
hearing of it. There!—don't
mind the sum at all; I can get
Bessy Crosby or Mary Dooley
to do it, and thank me for
asking; or Miss Moriarty won't
mind it; for I can wind her
round my finger, as often as I
like, by asking her to tell me

about her father, the Captain——"

"Hush, sister! hush!" in-
terrupted May, in her turn;
"don't let any one hear you
speak that way; for I am
sure you do not mean it. If
you require help, I am always
ready to give it so far as I
can; and if Miss Moriarty
sometimes speaks of her father, we ought to remember
that she has suffered much,
and that——"

"You are a good creature,

May," once more interrupted Aileen, throwing her arm round her sister's neck, and kissing her; "and though you scold me oftener than all of them put together, I believe you are dearer to me than any."

And so it was, and so it ever will be. Pleasant friends and acquaintances, who overlook our faults or encourage our errors, are not the landmarks to which the true spirit clings, or the heart turns in

its moments of trouble, or even
of calmer thought. When we
look back on life, our softer
and better memories remember with gratitude and respect
not those who indulged, but
those who restrained us,—
those who prayed that we
might avoid temptation, rather than those who led us
into it themselves,—those, in
fine, who taught us that life
is short and eternity long,
rather than such as by their
precepts or example endea-

voured to make us forget that
we hold our fate in our own
hands, and that although
free will is given us, it is not
to pervert its uses or abuse
the liberty graciously vouch-
safed to us by a good God, in
order to become the instru-
ments and agents of His
direst foe.

For some years, and while
they continued to be mere
children, things went smooth-
ly and pleasantly enough with
"the Rose." She had a ready

wit, a pretty face, and too in-
dulgent friends, and she was
thus enabled to gloss over her
ignorance, while her faults
were forgiven or forgotten by
those who could have con-
quered them, but did not,
until they became so deeply
imbedded as to make those
tremble for her future who
were really interested in her
fate. The world had pros-
pered with her father, too;
and as he was now beginning
to accumulate wealth, lived

in a larger house, and formed
new acquaintances and friends,
of a rank superior to his old,
his eldest daughter's foibles
became more and more mani-
fest every day, and she became
more confirmed in her disin-
clination to submit to any
check but that of her own
will. Neither was her choice
of companions what it ought
to have been: the vain, the
frivolous, the extravagant,
and the sycophantic, were
those whom she most encour-

aged and consorted with; and, although Kitty sometimes ventured to counsel her, the advice of so feeble an advocate was disregarded, whilst May's more serious entreaties were treated sometimes with anger, and always with contempt. She had now in some degree outgrown Miss Moriarty's tuition; or, at least, she had expressed to her father a wish to give up going to school; and, as he called her "his little housekeeper," and had a

notion that women required
little learning, he indulged
her in that, as he did in every
thing else, and was quite content to see her pleased and
happy, without inquiring, as
he ought to have done, whe-
ther she deserved to be so.
Indeed, even if he had done
so, he would have found it
difficult to arrive at the truth;
Kitty Neill was both too fond
of and too much under the control of her imperious "Rose"
to speak a syllable in her

dispraise; and the humbler "Lily" was never questioned, and would never have thought of annoying her father's mind by telling him of faults which she was sanguine enough to hope would be rectified by time and thought. Besides, May did not by any means know the entire extent of her sister's folly, or how far her love of pleasure and admiration led her. She was aware that Aileen gained credit for many things to which she never ap-

3

plied her mind or put her hand, and that the good "housekeeping," of which her father was so proud, owed its perfection to herself; she knew also that during her father's absence her sister was easily enticed away, to walk, to visit, or to shop, by companions like herself, who found home irksome, and who thought every occupation unwelcome, save such as had pleasure and idleness for its end and aim; but she *did* not

know that Aileen had been
reduced to mean and un-
worthy shifts in order to sus-
tain her in her extravagance.
Thus, her father gave into
her charge a certain sum per
month for the purpose of
"keeping the house," as it is
called; and, although it was
amply sufficient for such purpose, she did not use it as it
ought to have been used, in
paying the house-bills regu-
larly, but thoughtlessly squan-
dered portions of it in the

purchase of trinkets, ribands,
and unnecessary dress, un-
known to her father, leaving
the butcher, the baker, the
dairyman, and green-grocer
unpaid,—at least, in part,—
and condescending to tell lies,
and implicate her father's
credit and character, by saying that it was his want of
money, and not her want of
principle, which created the
delay. No doubt, she always
intended to pay those bills,
but still each month brought

its own temptations and its own demands, and, like all those who outrun their means, she felt that what looked possible enough when considered at a distance became quite impossible when it had in reality to be met.

Meantime, the modest and unobtrusive "Lily" grew and strengthened in body and mind. May mourned over her sister's infatuation, and her father's blindness to it; but sincerely loving Aileen, as she

did, she could not find in her
heart either to denounce her
openly, or even to dare her
anger for the sake of her soul.
In private she mourned with
Kitty over the altered habits
and more serious weaknesses of
"the Rose;" but when in her
presence, she was silent, partly
through affection, and partly
through fear; and when spo-
ken to about her by others,
she defended her, in the hope
that she would appreciate her

feelings when reason returned hereafter.

But, thoughtless as she was, she was soon to be awakened from dreams of indolence and pleasure to a sad and dark reality, for which she was altogether unprepared. In superintending the roof of a new building which he had been engaged to construct, a part of it, on which he stood, suddenly gave way, and Laurence MacMullen was carried home to his orphan daughters,

—a corpse. At first the poor girls could hardly comprehend the extent of their misfortune, and Aileen still less than May; they both loved their father, although in a different degree,—Aileen because he indulged her, and May because she felt that he was entitled to her dutiful respect; and now to be thus terribly and instantaneously deprived of his protection, rendered them powerless to act, to think, to feel, or, for the present, to do any thing but weep. In their sudden bereavement, however, they were not without friends to act for them, to whom his memory was dear; and during the subsequent scenes of sorrow, more than one kind hand was stretched forth to assist them and save them trouble. But, by-and-by, this good-natured excitement subsided; their parent was buried, and the question now to be seriously considered and debated was, "How were they to live?" Although MacMullen was beginning to thrive, still he had not had time to accumulate much, and, taken away suddenly as he had been, with work unfinished, contracts unfulfilled, and debts unsettled, it was difficult to settle his affairs, or, in effect, to arrive at a correct knowledge of how he stood with the world at all. Had the matter rested altogether with Aileen, it would have been a

hopeless business indeed; but
with May it was otherwise.
In his hurried moments, her
father had often employed
her to look over accounts,
and sometimes to post his
books, tot his memoranda,
and arrange his papers; and
now, when his executor and
friend, David O'Reilly, de-
manded to see and overlook
his accounts, she was able to
give him great assistance, and
not only that, but to point
out to him the easiest and

best mode of adjustment for
all. But, when all was done,
the sum total was far, very
far under what the sanguine
"Rose" had anticipated it
would be. Barely a hundred
pounds remained after the
payment of all just debts,
and of this nearly ten had
to go to liquidate the *private*
claims which milliners, per-
fumers, and others, brought
against the giddy and inconsiderate girl who was thus
hurled from comparative afflu-

ence and compelled to con-
sider how henceforth she was
to earn her own bread. Still,
however, she trusted that
those who had so often court-
ed her acquaintance and ap-
peared to delight in her society would not desert her
now, and that, one way or
other, they would invite her
to their homes, and provide
for her wants; but her experience of life was small indeed, or it would have told
her that those who court us

for what we have to give, are
not likely to inconvenience
themselves when we can give
no more, and that as rats
desert a falling house, and
swallows wing their way to
warmer regions when winter
approaches, so do the companions of the idle desert the
idle, and so do the bonds of
good-fellowship which linked
them together dissolve, at the
first frosts of misfortune or
sorrow.

At length the time came

when something must be done,
and as Aileen still loitered on
in the hope that something or
other (she did not know what)
might "turn up" in her favour, on May devolved the
unpleasant task of awaken-
ing her from her visions and
bringing her back to the world
of reality which stared them
in the face. She chose her
time, of an evening when her
sister had been out almost all
day visiting, and when she
had bitterly complained of

the slights she had met from
those who once received and
treated her in a very different
fashion.

"I am glad you have spo-
ken on the subject, Aileen,"
said May, " because it will
show you how idle are the
expectations you entertained
of being received and pro-
vided for by those who have
so treated you, and that it
would be better at once to
give up such vain hopes and
endeavour to provide for your-

self, as I mean immediately
to do. Our father has been
dead three months, and the
means in our hands cannot
last forever: had I been able
to arrange his affairs in less
time, I would both have
looked out for a situation
myself, and advised you to
do so before, and, as it is, I
think the sooner we set about
it the better. God always
assists those who are willing
to assist themselves, and, poor
and unprotected as we are at

5

present, He can and will raise
us up friends and better pros-
pects, if we only pray for a
continuance of His grace and
walk by the light of His
divine law."

"But what *can* I do, May?"
asked "the Rose," in a sub-
dued and startled tone.

"As to myself," continued
May, calmly, "I am better
qualified to face the world
than you are, Aileen, and
therefore I am more anxious
to provide for you than for

myself. I intend to advertise
for a situation as governess in
a Catholic family, as I think
I am quite competent to edu-
cate the junior branches, at
all events : I am afraid, however, that you could not venture to undertake so much,
and therefore I do not advise
you to try. It may be that
some of our well-wishers may
hear of a situation which
would suit you, as companion
to a lady, as I hear that such
are occasionally required by

persons of delicate health
who cannot be left alone. If
you think that such a situation would suit you, the sooner
we set about looking for it
the better. Dean Kennedy
met me only yesterday, and
asked me what we purposed
to do for the future; and as he
suggested to me the plan I
have mentioned for you, and
desired me to ask you about
it, it is possible he may have
something of the kind in view.
He told me he would call this

evening to speak to us both:
so that it would be wise to.
be prepared with an answer,
as he likes a plain one."

In about half an hour, and
while they were yet debating
about their affairs and pros-
pects, a knock at the door
announced a visitor, and Dean
Kennedy was ushered in. He
was a tall, stout, dignified,
and good-humoured looking
ecclesiastic, and, in reality,
was one of the most benevolent and kindly-hearted men

that ever lived. He extended
a hand to each of the girls,
and gave them his blessing
as he did so: he then sat
down, and addressed them in
his good-natured way.

"I come as the harbinger
of good tidings to you both,"
he said, "as I have succeeded
in obtaining a situation for
each, such as I think will
answer you for the present,
and lead to better things hereafter. For you, May, I have
done more than I have been

able to accomplish for your sister, because you are better prepared. Lady O'Donnell has consented to take you as governess to her younger daughters, and as Sir Francis, her husband, keeps a splendid establishment, and has a large connection, I look upon your lot as a particularly fortunate one. You are very young, to be sure, for so responsible a position, but I judge of you by your acts, and not by your age, and I have no fears for

your future, since you have
so well performed your part
in the past. As to you, my
poor child," he continued, addressing Aileen, with a graver
air, "I regret to say that I
have not been quite so suc-
cessful. Your sister's superior information, and greater
attention to her education,
give her advantages which,
unfortunately, you do not pos-
sess. There are two or three
families in which I could have
placed you in the same posi-

tion as that in which May
will be introduced to, but, of
course, as you have not the
necessary training or information, both for your sake and
my own, I could not recom-
mend you; failing in that,
however, I have done what I
hope will be advantageous to
you, in procuring for you the
situation of companion to Mrs.
Fitzgerald, an old and delicate
lady, who, although a little
eccentric in habit and manner (but we cannot have

every thing we wish, you
know), is in the main very
amiable, kindly, and well dis-
posed. She requires a young
person to read to and be constantly about her, and although this will include a
good deal of confinement and
some privation, still, as you
have not fitted yourself to
accept any thing higher, it
will, I hope, be acceptable
to you, and may serve as
an introduction to something
pleasanter, and more advan-

tageous, at a future day, for which, in the mean time, you may be preparing yourself, as I trust you will do. The salary will be small, but progressive, and, at all events, as you are not qualified to accept a more responsible situation, you must endeavour to be content with it."

At this announcement the misguided "Rose" felt in her inmost heart how little the ambition and love of pleasure and pleasant companions had

done for her, and how much
wiser her sister had been in
quietly remaining at home,
assisting her father and im-
proving her own mind. But,
as yet, the true spirit had not
visited her, and she felt only
annoyance and mortification
at the superior advantages
offered to May, and, if she
dared, would have rejected
the situation offered to herself with disdain. But Dean
Kennedy was not a man to
be trifled with, and as he had

always evinced an interest in their welfare, and had now evidently taken some trouble on their account, she had no reasonable excuse for refusing what he proposed, more especially as she was perfectly conscious that however much she might desire a higher position, still that it was her own deficiency which forbade her to aspire to it, or him to obtain it for her. It was a lesson of life, however, which was not lost upon her, young and thoughtless as she was, for in her own mind she silently determined to turn over a new leaf, and hereafter to turn her time to a better account than she had hitherto done.

In a few days, every thing was arranged, and for the first time in their lives the sisters were parted, and poor Kitty Neill, to her great grief, obliged to seek another home.

CHAPTER II.

Lady O'Donnell's reception of May MacMullen was both courteous and kind.

"I have heard the history of your life," she said, "from our mutual friend the Dean, and such is his high opinion of you, that I am not only willing to engage you, but happy in having an opportu-

63

nity of receiving you into my
family also. These young
ladies are to be your pupils:
their names **are** Emily, Jane,
and Elizabeth, and I trust you
will find them as docile and
amenable as it is their duty
to be towards one whose
efforts are for their good, and
whose example ought to be
an inducement to them to do
their best in order to excel."

Thus kindly received and
treated, May at once entered
upon her new vocation with

her accustomed earnestness
and zeal. It was now she
found that "the rewards of
labour are always sweet," as
she was enabled, without difficulty or trouble to herself, to
convey to her pupils the information of which her own
mind was full, and which she
had taken pains to accumulate in the very best way.
Indeed, before three months
had passed away, the value
of her system was seen, and,
while the parents of her pu-

pils were astonished at their
progress, the young people
themselves gratefully acknow-
ledged that it was to their
governess the merit was due,
for, as Emily, the youngest,
said to her mamma, "it was
impossible not to understand
what Miss MacMullen meant,
she had such a plain way of
saying and doing things, and
took such pains to explain
all that was necessary in the
shortest and best manner."
As a resident, too, May gave

equal satisfaction to those
under whose roof she was,
and to all connected with
them; quiet, humble, and
considerate in disposition and
manner, she was attentive
without being intrusive, and
courteous without servility;
accustomed to wait on herself,
she gave no trouble to servants, but on the contrary,
when visitors were in the
house, or company expected,
she placed herself at the ser-
vice of any one who required

assistance, and often made
herself so generally useful
that at length Lady O'Donnell learned to look upon her
as a confidential friend, rather
than any thing else, and
treated her as such, not alone
in private, but even in pub-
lic and when surrounded by
friends and associates of the
highest rank. Neither did
any one who knew her envy
her this distinction, for every
one was aware that she deserved it, and only used the

favour she enjoyed in order
to benefit others rather than
herself. A more unostenta-
tiously charitable pair did not
exist than Sir Francis O'Donnell and his lady, and, as
their almoner, the gentle May
was often despatched on mis-
sions of mercy, to shed balm
on wounded and weary hearts,
and her aid was often re-
quired in order to find out
deserving objects as well as
to relieve them. In point of
fact, her father's death, so far

from being an injury or misfortune to her, had been altogether otherwise; but this was attributable to herself,— to her own admirable good sense, which had made her not only see the right path, but stick to it, even at a time when the world looked prosperous and no one could have anticipated that she would have been so suddenly deprived of her protector and thrown on her own resources for a means of earning her bread.

Having thus far accompanied "the Lily" on her pleasant path, we will now turn to "the Rose," whose career was by no means so unruffled. Mrs. Fitzgerald, the lady with whom she was to live, was somewhat of a *malade imaginaire;* that is, one who supposed herself the victim of diseases, from which, except in imagination, she was totally free, but the fear of which,

nevertheless, tormented not
only herself, but every one
about her. She required con-
stant attendance, and per-
petual sympathy; expected to
find every thing ready for her
the moment she asked for it;
and thought far too much of
her own requirements to spare
the labour or time of those
who served her. She lived
in an atmosphere of medicine,
and was constantly hurrying
from one doctor to another
when any new symptom pre-

sented itself, or trying new
nostrums recommended in advertisements as infallible cures
for every disease, but which
she always said, with a sigh,
"never did *her* the least good."
Always weak and nervous, she
was perpetually "strengthen-
ing herself" with stimulating
food and wine, which inter-
fered with her digestion, and
made her still worse than she
was before; and, indolent by
nature and habit, she lingered
in bed until noon, took hardly

any exercise during the day,
and then wondered that she
could not sleep, and required
the presence of some one in
her room always to a late
hour, to listen to her com-
plaints, give her the medicine to which she continually
resorted, and endeavour to
amuse or console her, as the
case might be. It was to this
lady Aileen MacMullen was
introduced by the benevolent
Dean, who met the captious
inquiries and remarks of the

nervous lady in a very cheerful, off-handed, and satisfac-
tory way, although "the Rose"
trembled at the idea of all
that was expected of her by
one who seemed to have no
consideration for any human
being but herself.

"She is very young, my
dear Dean Kennedy," said
Mrs. Fitzgerald, on first seeing
her, "and not very strong-
looking, either: now, I remark
that very young girls are apt
to fall asleep just when I am

at the worst and most want them to keep awake; and then, if they are not strong, they begin to complain of sickness, and that upsets me dreadfully,—shatters my nerves, in fact, and makes me uncomfortable for days and days after. What is her name, you say?"

"Aileen MacMullen."

"Absurd! Aileen! how could I ever remember such an out-of-the-way name as that? But no matter; I can call her Ally, short, and that will answer. Can you read well, Ally?"

Aileen answered that she could.

"I am afraid you are very fond of dress, and I don't like any one about me that is," continued the lady, looking at her; "it takes up so much time, and I am always so poorly that I can't bear to be left alone; besides, I particularly require humility, and I detest vanity. I hope you

know how to give medicine
without making mistakes?"

Aileen answered, that she
would do her best.

"Yes, but you must be *sure*
of it; don't give yourself that
undecided way of speaking,
because it looks as if you
were afraid of doing right,
and so I might be poisoned,
you know. I hope her tem-
per is good, Mr. Dean!"

The Dean smiled, and said
he hoped so too.

"I am very particular in

the article of temper, Ally,"
she went on, addressing the
poor humbled "Rose;" "very
particular, indeed; my last
serious attack of congestion
was brought on by the ill-
temper of a young person who
attended me, and I might
say that the whole of my ill-
ness has been produced by
some such trials, for which
I never give any reasonable
cause, so that if you cannot
depend on your own temper,
I had rather you would not

engage with me at all. I
suppose you know how to
make jellies and custards: I
am fond of them, and the
doctors say they are good for
me; and sometimes, I dare
say, I would prefer your
making them to having them
cooked in the kitchen; besides, a young person who
has to earn her bread ought
to learn every thing, and
never be above putting her
hand to any thing. I should
like you to wear caps, too, or,

at all events, not to have so
many curls and things hang-
ing about your shoulders; indeed, I wonder your own good
sense wouldn't tell you how
unbecoming and improper
they are; but, by-and-by, we
can correct all that; and now
you may go down-stairs for a
little, and take off your bon-
net and shawl, as I shall want
you to give me two table-
spoonfuls of my restorative car-
diac-antispasmodic mixture almost immediately, and if I

don't take it at the regular
period, I cannot take my tonic
syrup and antiflatulent pills
in due course."

From the glimpse we have
thought it necessary to give
the reader of Aileen's new
employer, it will at once be
seen that her situation did
not promise to be a sinecure,
and a week's trial proved to
her that it was even more
difficult and troublesome than
she feared it could be. Her
eccentric mistress had a thou-

sand oddities, some one of
which was sure to turn up at
the most untoward times and
in the most extraordinary
way. At daylight she would
frequently call for coffee, or
soup, or wine and water, or
send for a physician, and keep
every one doing something or
other about her until he came.
Then, there were medicines
to be given, and lotions to be
applied, and symptoms to be
watched for or anticipated,
and when ease had been pro-

cured, she must be soothed, and read to, and consoled, and sometimes even sung to, when her spirits were particularly low. A single word uttered above the breath was sure to bring on what she called "a paroxysm," during which she alternately scolded, wept, and remonstrated, as if she were pleading for her life, or threatening a criminal with vengeance for attempting to take it. To sum up all, too, she was by no means generous

to any one but herself, and,
although her own dietary was
of the most costly and luxu-
rious kind, she thought that
the humblest and most meagre
fare ought to suffice those to
whom she gave so much trouble, and from whom she expected so much.

Completely opposed as all
this was to Aileen MacMullen's former habits and mode
of life, she found it at first
almost intolerable, and she
would have given it up in

disgust, had she not been for-
tified by the admonitions of
the good Dean, who conjured
her to receive her present
sufferings as a penance for her
former forgetfulness, and to
endeavour to bear with them
for a time, in order to pre-
pare her for better things
hereafter; she was also consoled and encouraged to per-
severe by the affectionate let-
ters of, and meetings with,
May, who wrote to her frequently, and saw her once,

and frequently twice, a week.
The considerate "Lily" did
not annoy her by contrasting
their lots in life, but rather
endeavoured to inspirit her to
bear the annoyances she was
now meeting with fortitude,
and at every leisure moment
to attend to those studies
which might serve to raise
her out of them, if she per-
severed as she ought. For-
tunately, too, those reasonable
and seasonable arguments,
coming as they did from those

whom she well knew to be
full of interest and affection
for her, fell on a spirit softened
rather than hardened by what
she was now obliged to bear,
and made her listen to them
respectfully, and treasure them
as her best guides for a course
to be adopted for the future.
Heretofore, and when prosperity and pleasure surrounded her, she had been by no
means as observant even of
her religious duties as she
should be, and now her first

reformatory steps were in that direction; she frequented the Blessed Sacraments frequently, she prayed often and fervently to the divine Mother, and the sainted servants of God, to intercede for her, that grace might be given her to redeem her errors and atone for her sins, and she curbed her waywardness of temper, and struggled hard to bear with the exactions and inconsiderate demands of the invalid whom she found it so hard to please. In the main, however, Mrs. Fitzgerald was not an unfeeling woman, when her "nerves" permitted her to think of others as well as herself: she had, within a year or two, made trial of several young persons, some of whom were pert, some sullen, and all of whom grew tired of her whims, and at last deserted her, and now that she had met with one superior to most of them, and humble and more forbearing than any,

she began, after a time, to
grow more considerate herself, and to forbear exacting
as much as she used to do,
except at intervals, and when
her "paroxysms" obliged her,
in despite of her better nature, to give way. Besides,
as long threatening comes at
last, her health, *in reality,*
began seriously to decline,
and she found the great com-
fort of having a well-informed
and cheerful attendant about
her, who was actuated by

principle in soothing her sufferings and supplying her
wants. To Aileen herself
this discipline of the mind
was advantageous in every
way, and when at last, and
after a whole year of suffer-
ing, Mrs. Fitzgerald and her
ills, real and affected, depart-
ed, it was in the arms of the
now altered "Rose" she died,
and hers was the prayer for
mercy and peace which she
last asked, for and seemed
most pleased to hear. This

was a reward, and a very
great one, too, to the young
girl, for her attention and
care; but the good will and
grateful feeling of the invalid
were proved in a yet more
substantial form, for on open-
ing her will it was found that
Aileen MacMullen had been
left three hundred pounds as
a mark of grateful affection
by one whose sufferings she
had soothed, and whose death-
bed she had contributed to
make easy.

"You see, my dear child," said the Dean, "that out of evil springs good, and that we were all right in doing as we have done,—you in bearing the inconveniences which you felt so grievous at first, and your sister and I in advising you to do so. But your trial is yet to come, and this comparatively large sum of money may prove to you either a blessing or a curse, according as you use it. You have already had some slight expe-

rience of the hollow profes-
sions of those who call themselves your friends, and I
trust that you will remember
how they have acted towards
you, and make a happier and
more sensible choice of associates for the time to come."

But "the Rose" had already
settled her plans, and only
waited to receive her legacy
in order to commence them.
She was still young,—not
much more than eighteen,—
and, with May's concurrence,

she took lodgings as near to her sister's residence as she could, and there, in silence and privacy, she recommenced her education, providing herself with masters, and diligently pursuing the studies which they recommended. When it became known that she had been left a "fortune,"—which report greatly increased, as it always does,—many of her former butterfly friends sought her out, or endeavoured to attract her notice as she met

them in the street. But she
felt no temptation to alter her
present plans or resume her
old career; so that, although
she accosted them civilly, and
received them courteously
when they called, she showed
them by her manner that the
old spirit had altogether de-
parted, and that a new and
better one had taken its place.
To say the truth, however, on
the score of society she had
no need to fall back on those
who had looked coldly on her

when attentions might have
been of use, since the high
consideration in which "the
Lily" was held by the O'Donnell family extended itself to
her, and she was admitted
not only to visit her sister at
all times, but frequently in-
vited to spend days at their
house among the happy family
group. The good Dean, al-
ways her friend, had told them
her history in full, and they
honored her for the struggles
she had made against the

faults and weaknesses which
had so long beset her, and
honoured her still more for
the judicious way in which
she was now using her money
and her time. Thus incited
to perseverance on all hands,
she labored hard to prove
herself worthy of the regard
in which she was held; and
after about eighteen months,
spent in preparation, she felt
herself fully competent to undertake the charge of pupils,
and at once commenced her

search of them. So judicious-
ly had she used her legacy
that more than two hundred
pounds remained to her, which
she treasured up for a rainy
day, or reserved as a fund to
be devoted as prudence might
direct. As her character and
qualifications now stood high
with all who knew her, after
a short time she had many
engagements, and all of the
most respectable kind, to ful-
fil, and gradually her fame as
a teacher became so high that

many of the parents of her best pupils solicited her to extend her usefulness, and open a seminary, where, with less labour to herself, she might receive a much larger number of scholars and a better income. At first, the idea of undertaking any thing so responsible daunted her; but, on referring the proposal to her always kind director the Dean, he said that he thought the thing might be done, and ought to be done,—but on one condition, namely, that her sister, May, would join her in it.

"Singly," he said, "either of you might fail ; but when united, I have no fear for the result. I am not an advocate for partnerships, except where mutual affection tightens the bonds of mutual interest, and creates a double motive to keep all right. Besides, May, I dare say, has a little hoard of her own, which, added to yours, would make a respectable capital to begin with."

"But should I be right, sir, to ask May to leave a situation where she is so much looked up to and loved, merely to oblige and serve me?" said Aileen.

"You forget that it will oblige and serve herself also," replied the Dean, with a smile; "her pupils at Lady O'Donnell's are now grown up, and in a short time she would have to look for another situation, which might not happen to be as pleasant as her present one. A home of her own will, therefore, be a more natural and more agreeable retreat."

"But May may not like to join me, sir," persisted Aileen; "she may remember my former faults, and have her fears that I might become as careless and giddy as I was before."

"Hardly, I should think," was the answer; "your former errors were those of an inex-

perienced girl, who had no
mother to advise or control
her, and who fell into the
hands of those who were ill
qualified for so grave and responsible an office as they
undertook.   But you have
been tried by the tests both
of adversity and prosperity
since then, and your conduct,
while so tempted, is a sufficient guarantee that you
have learned wisdom in the
school of experience, and may
now venture to undertake the

guidance both of others and yourself."

Thus encouraged, Aileen opened her proposals to May at their next meeting, telling her that she had no desire to influence her unless the proposition met her own entire concurrence, and unless, on consideration, she thought it would be for their mutual good.

"It is singular enough," was May's cheerful answer, "and I hope it may be ominous of

good, that just such a scheme
as you now propose has been
running through my brain for
some time, and I only hesi-
tated to speak about it, lest
you should dislike it, or think
that it might bind you too
much. Indeed, it was first
suggested to me by Lady
O'Donnell herself, as the girls
are now grown up and will
not require my services any
longer, and my kind friends
would not wish to part with
me unless they knew that in

doing so I would be at least
as comfortable as I have been
with them. As to funds, we
shall be splendidly off; be-
tween us we can make up five
or, it may be, six hundred
pounds, and after taking and
furnishing our house, with
God's blessing, the residue
will be more than sufficient
to meet our expenses and
keep us out of debt until we
see how our new speculation
may answer."

After a warm sisterly embrace, "the Rose" and "the Lily" parted, soon again to be once more united and dwelling under the same roof. But different, indeed, was it from the residence of their earlier years. In May there was nothing to be corrected; she had never yielded to temptation, and had never suffered the after-penalty which is sure to visit those who do; the world's respect had followed her, for God's grace surrounded her, as a shield and safe-

guard, and thus protected she
had always walked secure.
With her sister it had been
different : flattered and fooled
by those who ought to have
known better, her weaker
mind perceived not the hol-
lowness and want of good
sense in such adulation, and
she received it at first as a
compliment, and finally as
her due. Her father's death
dissipated these dangerous
thoughts and feelings, and
showed her how perilous it is

to trust for friendship or support to those who foster our foibles and are careless of our real respectability and good name. She had been tried and had triumphed, and now she was about to receive her reward, in the most pleasing and profitable way. After various consultations, and much thought, a house was taken, furniture procured, masters engaged, advertisements put forth, and, by the influence and exertions of Sir

Francis O'Donnell and Dean
Kennedy, the twin sisters
commenced operations, with
a class of six boarders, all of
the highest respectability, and
on the most advantageous
terms. In fact, from that day
forth they prospered exceedingly, and their character,
after a very short period,
stood so high that they were
obliged to decline the reception of pupils rather than to
solicit them, in compliance
with a rule established at

May's wise suggestion from the first, namely, never to take a single scholar more than they might be able to have under their own personal care and supervision, and for whose progress they could not undertake to be personally answerable. This rule, although it restricted them as to numbers, added considerably to the character of their school, and for many years their establishment has been now of the very first

8

class, and "the Rose" and "the Lily" have acquired both competence and fame.

In conclusion, we think it useful to say that the principal incidents of this little history are literally true, and we have written it in order to show that at no period of life is it safe to forget principle, or depart, even in the slightest degree, from the dictates of probity and truth.

THE END.

CATALOGUE

OF

CATHOLIC BOOKS

PUBLISHED BY

H. McGRATH,

733 Market Street, Philadelphia.

Booksellers, Clergymen, Religious Societies, and others, purchasing for sale or gratuitous distribution, will be allowed a liberal discount from the annexed prices.

Baxter's Most Important Tenets of the Catholic Church. 32mo. Half bound, 13 cents. Cloth, 19 cents.

Catholic Pocket Library. By St. Alphonsus Liguori. In 3 vols., 32mo. Cloth, 25 cents each.

Catholic Doctrine proved from Scripture and Tradition. 18mo. Cloth, 38 cents.

Caroline Henson; or, The Pious Orphan Girl. 32mo. Half bound, 13 cents. Cloth, 19 cents.

Catholic Sunday-School Hymn-Book. 32mo. Paper, 6 cents. Half bound, 13 cents.

Catholic Sunday-School Hymn-Book and Sacred Melodies. 24mo. Half bound, 25 cents.

Cottage Conversations. Conversations on the Doctrines and Practices of the Catholic Church. 18mo. Cloth, 50 cents.

Devotions to the Sacred Heart of Jesus. 18mo. Price, from 50 cents to $2.00.

Eleanor Mortimer; or, The World and the Cloister. By Agnes M. Stewart. 18mo. Cloth, 50 cents.

Edith Mortimer; or, The Trials of Life. By Mrs. Parsons. 18mo. Cloth, 50 cents.

Exercise of Faith. Impossible except in the Catholic Church. 18mo. Cloth, 38 cents.

Faith, Hope, and Charity. A Tale of the Reign of Terror. 12mo. Cloth, 75 cents.

Fourfold Difficulty of Anglicanism. By J. Spencer Northcote, M.A. 18mo. Cloth, 38 cents.

Form of Consecration of a Bishop. By the Most Rev. F. P. Kenrick, D.D. 18mo. Paper cover, 13 cents.

Father Drummond and his Orphans; or, The Children of Mary. 18mo. Cloth, 38 cents.

Good Child's Own Book. Square 16mo, with numerous illustrations. Cloth, 50 cents.

Good Child's Story-Book. Square 16mo, with numerous illustrations. Cloth, 50 cents.

Gospels for the Sundays and Festivals. 32mo. Paper cover, 6 cents. Half bound, 13 cents.

Growth in Holiness; or, The Progress of the Spiritual Life. By F. W. Faber, D.D. 12mo. Cloth, 75 cents.

Hell Opened to Christians to Caution them from Entering into it. 32mo. Half binding, 13 cents. Cloth, 19 cents.

Instructions on the Holiness and Dignity of the Sacrament of Matrimony. 18mo. Cloth, 38 cents.

Life of the Blessed Virgin Mary, Mother of God. To which are added, the Life of St. Ann, and of St. Margaret, Queen of Scotland. 18mo. Half bound, 19 cents. Cloth, 25 cents.

Life of St. Theresa. To which is added, the Life of St. Mary, of Egypt. 32mo. Cloth, 25 cents.

Lives of the Blessed Virgin, St. Ann, St. Margaret, and St. Liguori. In one volume, 18mo. Cloth, 38 cents.

Life of St. Alphonsus Liguori. 18mo. Half bound, 19 cents. Cloth, 25 cents.

Little Manual of Confession; or, Guide to Grace. 32mo. Paper cover, 6 cents. Cloth, 13 cents.

Life of Father Ephraim and his Sister, Religious of La Trappe. 12mo. Cloth, 75 cents.

Louisa Warden: a Catholic Tale. 32mo. Paper, 6 cents. Cloth, 13 cents.

Mary, the Morning Star; or, A Model of Interior Life. 24mo. Cloth, 38 cents.

Meditations for every Day in the Year, on the Principal Duties of Christianity. By Père Griffet, S.J. 32mo. Cloth, 38 cents.

Moral Tales for My Young Countrymen. By J. C. Sherlock, Esq. 18mo. Cloth, 37½ cents.

Novena to St. Anthony. 24mo. Paper, 13 cents.

Path of Perfection. Purifying, illuminating, and uniting. 18mo. Cloth, 50 cents.

Preston Hall. A Catholic House in 1580 and 1855. A Tale. 16mo. Cloth, 50 cents.

Protestant's Objections on Controverted Points of Faith by the Written Word. 18mo. Cloth, 38 cents.

Rose of Tanenbourg. A Moral Tale. By Canon Schmid. 18mo. Cloth, 38 cents.

Rudiments of Singing. By Professor Pique. 24mo. Paper, **6 cents.**

St. Liguori's Spiritual Works. Being a Selection from the larger Works of St. Alphonsus Liguori. 32mo. Cloth, 50 cents.

Sinner's Guide. **By** the **Rev. F.** Lewis, of Grenada. 12mo. Cloth, 75 cents.

Sister Camilla, the Carmelite; or, The Life and Times of Mad. Soyecourt. 18mo. Cloth, 50 cents.

Speech of the Hon. J. R. Chandler, on the Temporal power of the Pope. 8vo. Paper, 13 cents.

Sinner's Conversion Reduced to Principles. By F. Francis Salazar, S.J. 24mo. Cloth, 31 cents.

Tales of the Sacraments. By Miss Agnew, authoress of Geraldine. 18mo. Cloth, 50 cents.

The Blessed Sacrament; or, The Works and Ways of God. By F. W. Faber, D.D. 18mo. Cloth, 50 cents.

The Month of Mary. Particularly adapted to the Month of May. By a member of the Ursuline Community. 24mo. Cloth, 37½ cents.

The Glories of Mary, Mother of God. By St. Alphonsus Liguori. 24mo. Cloth, 37½ cents.

The Glories of Mary, Mother of God. A cheap edition. 32mo. Cloth, 25 cents.

The Glories of Jesus, contemplated in the Mirror of Divine Love. 24mo. Cloth, 37½ cents.

The Glories of St. Joseph, Spouse of the Ever-Blessed Virgin. 24mo. Cloth, 37½ cents.

The Glories of the Holy Angels. Revised, improved, and corrected by a clergyman of Philadelphia. 24mo. Cloth, 37½ cents.

The Flower-Basket. A Catholic Tale, from the German of Canon Schmid. 18mo. Cloth, 38 cents.

Theobald; or, The Triumph of Charity. 16mo. Cloth, 50 cents.

Unity of the Episcopate Considered. By Edward Healy Thomson, M.A. 18mo. Cloth, 50 cents.

White's Confutation of Church-of-Englandism, and Correct Exposition of the Catholic Faith. 12mo. Cloth, 75 cents.

Young Catholic's Guide in the Preparation for Confession. 32mo. Paper cover, 6 cents.

PRAYER-BOOKS.

The Spirit of Prayer. A new Manual of Catholic Devotion. By a Member of the Ursuline Community, Cork. 18mo. Large type. In various bindings, at prices from 50 cents to $8.00.

The New Catholic Manual; and Pious Exercises for the Use of the Faithful. 24mo. In various bindings, at prices from 38 cents to $6.50.

The Spirit of Devotion; A Manual of Pious Exercises for Catholics; and the Mass, with Illustrations. Royal 32mo. In various bindings, at prices from 31 cents to $5.50.

Christian Guide to Heaven. A Manual of Spiritual

Exercises for Catholics. 32mo. In various bindings, at prices from 25 cents to $4.50.

Guide to Heaven; or, Daily Exercises. 48mo. In various bindings, at prices from 19 cents to $1.00.

Child's Own Prayer-Book. A Manual of Devotion for Young Catholic Children. 48mo. In various bindings, **at** prices from 15 to 88 cents.

Gems of Piety. A neat little pocket Prayer-Book. 64mo. In various bindings, at prices from 13 to 75 cents.

CATECHISMS.

Catechism of the Christian Doctrine. Prepared by order of the National Council, for the use of Catholics in the United States of America. 3 cents, or $1.75 per 100.

Catechism of the Christian Doctrine. Prepared by order of the National Council. Abridged from the larger one. 2 cents, or $1 per 100.

Catechism for First Confession. 32mo. Paper, 3 cents, or $2 per 100.

Catechism for Confirmation. 32mo. Paper, 3 cents, or $2 per 100.

Catechism for First Communion. Translated from the French, and revised by the Very Rev. Father Pagani. 32mo. Paper covers, 6 cents, or $4 per 100.

Catechism for Mass. Being an Easy and Simple Explanation of the Ceremonies and Prayers of the Holy Sacrifice. 32mo. Paper, 6 cents, or $4 per 100.

Butler's Large Catechism, 5 cents, or $3 per
100.

Butler's Small Catechism, 3 cents, or $1.50 per
100.

The Good Child's Library.

In 6 Volumes, Square 16mo.

Each volume sold separately, or in sets of six.
Fancy paper covers, 13 cents. Neat cloth, gilt
backs, 25 cents, containing

The Two Doves, and other Tales. A Story-Book
for the Young.

Harry Tripp; or, Shaking the Crab-Tree, and
other Stories for the Young.

The Clever Boy, and other Stories for the
Young.

The Little Basket-Maker, and other Stories for
the Young.

The Water Fairy, and other Stories for the
Young.

The King of the Swans, and other Stories for the
Young.

Parochial and Sunday-School Library.

In 12 Volumes, Square 24mo.   First Series.

Each volume sold separately, or in sets of twelve. Fancy paper covers, 15 cents; or in neat cloth, gilt backs, 25 cents. Containing

The Wonderful Doctor. An Eastern Tale. By Canon Schmid.

The Easter Eggs, and other Tales. In one vol. By Canon Schmid.

The Nightingale, and the Inundation of the Rhine. In one vol. By Canon Schmid.

Henry Eichenfels, and The Fire. In one vol. By Canon Schmid.

Hop-Blossoms, and The Cray-Fish. In one vol. By Canon Schmid.

The Jewels, and Diamond Ring. In one vol. By Canon Schmid.

The Wooden Cross, and Chapel of Wolfsbuhl. In one vol. By Canon Schmid.

Lewis, the Little Emigrant. By Canon Schmid.

The Little Hermit. By Canon Schmid.

Christmas Eve. By Canon Schmid.

The Black Lady, and other Tales. In one volume. By Canon Schmid.

Memoirs of a Guardian Angel. A Catholic Tale. Translated from the French.

Parochial and Sunday-School Library.

In 12 Volumes, Square 24mo. Second Series.

Each volume sold separately, or in sets of twelve. Fancy paper covers, 15 cents; or in neat cloth, gilt backs, 25 cents. Containing

Hail Mary; or, The Beauties of the **Angelican** Salutation. And other Tales.

Valentine Redmond; or, The Cross of the Forest. And other Tales. In one volume.

The Angel of Consolation. To which is added, The Infidel's Death-Bed. In one volume.

The Adopted Son. And other Tales. In one volume.

Isabella; or, The Heroine of Algiers. And other Tales. In one volume.

Lucy Lambert; or, The Shrine of the Forest. By Mary M. King.

Lent Lilies. And other Tales. In one volume.

Poor Fanny; or, The Motherless Child who found a Mother. By Mary Monica.

The Little Snow-Drop; or, The Unbaptized One. By Cecelia Mary Cadell.

The Step-Sisters; or, A Cure for Prejudice. And other Tales. In one volume.

Lucy Ward; or, The Dweller in the Tabernacle.

Rich and Poor; or, Lady Adela and Grumbling Molly.

Brother James's Library.

In 12 Volumes, Royal 32mo.

Each volume sold separately, or in sets of twelve. Fancy paper covers, 10 cents; or in neat cloth, gilt backs, 19 cents. Containing,

O'Hara Blake; or, The Lost Heir.

Clare Costelloe; A True Story.

The Two Friends; or, The Reward of Industry.

Catherine Hall; or, The Deserted Child.

Miles O'Donnell; or, The Story of a Life.

Little Mary; or, The Child of Providence.

The Cousins; or, The Test of Friendship.

The Bequest; or, All is not Gold that Glitters.

The Rose and the Lily; or, The Twin Sisters.

Rody O'Leary; or, The Young Outlaw.

The Village Ruin, and Knight of the Sheep.

The White Knight; or, The Rock of the Candle.

Catholic Pocket Library.

In 13 Volumes, 32mo.

A series of valuable little works. By **St. Alphon-sus Liguori.** Each volume sold separately, or in sets of thirteen. Paper covers, 6 cents. Cloth, 12 cents. Containing,

Divine Love, and the means of acquiring it.

Consolation and Encouragement for a Soul in a State of Spiritual Desolation, with admonitions for persons in every state of life.

Means of Acquiring Perfection.

Conformity with the Will of God.

Conversing Continually and Familiarly with God.

Practice of Meditation and Practice of Perfection.

Rules of a Christian Life.

Practice of Christian Virtues.

Obligation of Children and Parents towards each other.

Explanation of the Sacrament of Penance.

Novena to the Sacred Heart of Jesus.

The Virtue of Chastity, the Enormity of the Sin of Impurity, with remedies against this horrible vice.

The Injuries done to our Neighbor, in his Charac-ter, Person, Property, &c.

**This book is DUE on the last
date stamped below**

www.ingramcontent.com/pod-product-compliance
Lightning Source LLC
Chambersburg PA
CBHW031440280326
41927CB00038B/1246